Endless
Stars

Strip-Pieced Quilts That Sparkle

Jean M. Potetz

Martingale®
& C O M P A N Y

Endless Stars: Strip-Pieced Quilts That Sparkle
© 2004 by Jean M. Potetz

That Patchwork Place® is an imprint
of Martingale & Company®.

Martingale & Company
20205 144th Avenue NE
Woodinville, WA 98072-8478
www.martingale-pub.com

Printed in China
09 08 07 06 05 04   8 7 6 5 4 3 2 1

Library of Congress Cataloging-in-Publication Data

Potetz, Jean M.
  Endless stars / Jean M. Potetz.
    p. cm.
  ISBN 1-56477-505-4
  1. Patchwork—Patterns. 2. Quilting—Patterns. 3. Star quilts. 4. Stars in art. I. Title.
  TT835 . P674 2004
  746 . 46'041—dc22

                                                    2003016700

Mission Statement
Dedicated to providing quality products and service
to inspire creativity.

Credits

President: Nancy J. Martin

CEO: Daniel J. Martin

Publisher: Jane Hamada

Editorial Director: Mary V. Green

Managing Editor: Tina Cook

Technical Editor: Janet Wickell

Copy Editor: Karen Koll

Design and Production Manager: Stan Green

Illustrator: Laurel Strand

Cover and Text Designer: Regina Girard

Photographer: Brent Kane

Dedication

To Richard—who made *Endless Stars* possible

Acknowledgments

Heartfelt appreciation to my grandmother, Mae Dargie, who trusted me as a child with her little green Singer; my mother, Audrey McLarty, who always encouraged me and willingly bound large quilts under a short deadline; my daughter Andrea Potetz Wysocki, who helped fine-tune patterns and choose fabrics for my quilt "Summer Nights"; my son Brian, who brainstormed on the Endless Stars technique; my husband, Richard, who sparked my imagination and spent endless hours discussing Endless Stars; and my nephew Sean Haber, who pushed me to think outside the box.

Special thanks to Linda Kozlenko for her assistance with my manuscript and my quilts, and for her encouragement throughout this project and always; Nancy Derr for sharing her talent with color and for her support; my "Quilt Buddies" Jeanne Bennett-Russo, Janine Friedman, Kitty Kurpiewski, Debbie McKinniss, Lisa Salonia, Liz Tamiso, Emily Tamiso, Sue Varesio, and Terre Wenthe for their valued guidance and willingness to test my Endless Stars patterns; Wilma Cogliantry for her artistic talent as a machine quilter, her willingness to meet a tight publication deadline, and her words of wisdom; Mary Bagley for asking me to teach Endless Stars before I was ready; and Barbara Askew, who taught me perseverance. Many thanks also to my copy editor, Karen Koll, and my technical editor, Janet Wickell, for their valuable assistance. I couldn't have done this without all of you!

Contents

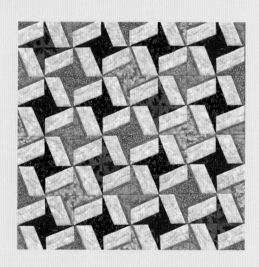

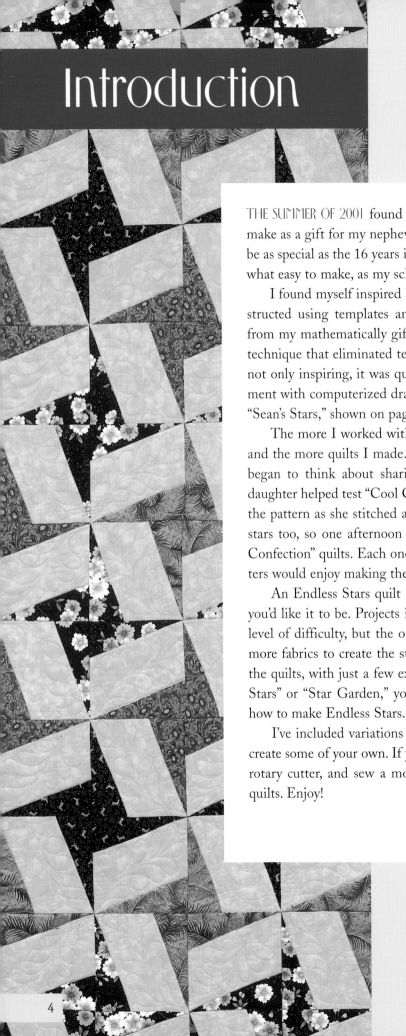

Introduction

THE SUMMER OF 2001 found me searching through books for a quilt to make as a gift for my nephew's birthday. And, while this quilt needed to be as special as the 16 years it was celebrating, it also needed to be somewhat easy to make, as my schedule was fairly full.

I found myself inspired by a four-pointed star pattern that was constructed using templates and traditional piecing methods. With help from my mathematically gifted husband, I came up with a strip-pieced technique that eliminated templates altogether. Now the Star block was not only inspiring, it was quick and easy. I used fabric scraps to experiment with computerized drawings and piecing formulas. The result was "Sean's Stars," shown on page 52.

The more I worked with the stars, the more variations I discovered and the more quilts I made. The possibilities seemed. . . well, endless. I began to think about sharing the technique with other quilters. My daughter helped test "Cool Confection" one Saturday, and we fine-tuned the pattern as she stitched along. My quilting friends wanted to try the stars too, so one afternoon we made "Kate's Endless Stars" and "Cool Confection" quilts. Each one was such a success that I knew other quilters would enjoy making these quilts.

An Endless Stars quilt is fun to make and as simple or complex as you'd like it to be. Projects in this book are arranged according to their level of difficulty, but the only variable that increases the level is using more fabrics to create the stars. The basic technique is the same for all the quilts, with just a few exceptions. If you begin with "Kate's Endless Stars" or "Star Garden," you'll acquire a good, basic understanding of how to make Endless Stars.

I've included variations to get you thinking, and I challenge you to create some of your own. If you can use a quilting ruler, cut fabric with a rotary cutter, and sew a mostly straight ¼" seam, you can make these quilts. Enjoy!

Jean M. Potetz

ENDLESS STARS ARE four-pointed stars that emerge when strip-pieced units are sewn together. The stars skip across the quilt top and continue multiplying as long as you keep adding units. Only a border or binding can stop them.

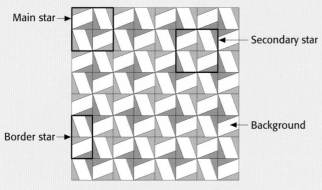

Endless Stars are composed of main stars, secondary stars, border stars, and a background.

■ Main star   ■ Secondary star

Quilt Elements

Endless Stars quilts contain two types of complete stars: main stars and secondary stars. A main star radiates from the center of four star units that are sewn together. Secondary stars are created when star units are sewn together in multiple rows. It is the secondary star that gives the appearance of continuing on and it is through this star that design variations become possible.

Border stars are the half stars that surround the outside edges of the quilt. They are incomplete secondary stars. The wide strips that separate main stars from secondary stars form the background.

Throughout the instructions, you will see references to horizontal star units and vertical star units. These layout designations help you arrange your rows correctly. The units are pieced in the same way and may look exactly alike—it's their orientation that makes them horizontal or vertical star units. All of the

projects in this book begin with a horizontal star unit in the upper-left corner.

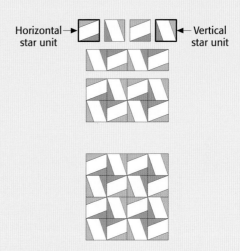

Horizontal star unit → ← Vertical star unit

Endless Stars Patterns

Every quilt in this book began as a gray-toned sketch of main stars and secondary stars. I colored the star units and background to create a design I liked, and then chose fabrics of similar shades to make my quilt.

While some projects appear to be assembled medallion style—from the center outward—or in diagonal rows, all of the quilts are constructed by sewing star units into horizontal rows, and then sewing the rows together.

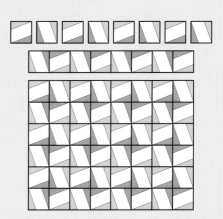

You can dramatically change a quilt's design by altering the placement of its colors and the values of its fabrics. Focus on fabrics that highlight the quilt's center and encircle it with rays of color to turn it into a medallion design, or make your stars flow in diagonal bands of color. These are just two of the endless variations possible.

Medallion-Style Variation

Diagonal Variation

Border-Star Design

You can create an interesting border by using the same fabric for border stars and borders. This gives the impression that the border extends into the quilt top. "Kate's Endless Stars" on page 21 and "Starshine" on page 33 are both examples of this technique. This type of border treatment works on any quilt that uses the same fabric for all of the border stars.

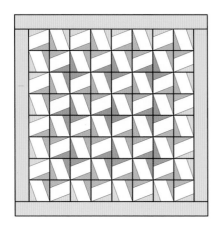

A different effect is created in a pattern such as "Summer Garden" on page 37, in which the border stars are sewn from multiple fabrics. A border made from any of the border-star fabrics would appear to move periodically into and out of the quilt top, creating a choppy appearance.

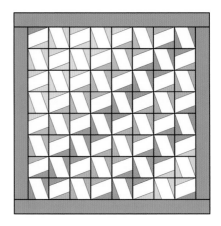

Introducing a new fabric for the border allows the border stars to remain part of the design.

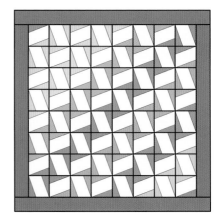

Now that you understand how Endless Stars are formed and how their designs are created, you're ready to begin. Read the section about choosing fabrics, pick a project, visit your favorite quilt shop, and start cutting. But beware—Endless Stars are addictive!

CONTRAST IS THE most important thing to remember when choosing fabrics for an Endless Stars quilt. You must consider how a fabric's color, value (light to dark), scale (print size), and visual texture (print style) interact with other fabrics. If you want your stars to stand out, there must be a sharp contrast between the stars and the background.

To make my stars sparkle, I usually like to use a background fabric that is lighter than the stars. Dark and bright colors are often noticed first, and while they make excellent stars, they can be overpowering when used as backgrounds. However, there are no rules, and I have seen dark backgrounds work very well.

I could fill a page with suggestions on choosing fabrics, but that might inhibit your creativity. Making Endless Stars should be fun, not something to worry about. Look at the quilts in the book. Notice the sharp contrast between the stars and backgrounds. Study the value, texture, and scale of the fabrics and then do what makes you happy—your stars will shine!

Which Fabric for Which Star?

Once you've chosen the fabrics for your stars, you need to decide if they will be main stars or secondary stars. Here are a few guidelines that always help me make that decision.

1. Stars in the four corners of the quilt are always main stars. Is there a fabric you'd like to feature there?
2. Is there a center star in the pattern? If so, is there a special fabric you would you like to use in that spot? Is it a main star or a secondary star?
3. Which fabrics would look best surrounding the outside edges of the pieced top? Use them for your border stars. Border stars are secondary stars.
4. Do you want to repeat a star fabric in your border? If so, do you want the border to be cut from the same fabric as the border stars?

While there is good color contrast between the large-scale floral and the moss green fabric, the visual texture of the green star is too busy, so it blends into the floral background, making the star disappear.

Here the almost-solid marbleized green creates a sharp line of contrast against the large-scale floral background and balances evenly with the open texture of the tone-on-tone purple. See the finished quilt, "Star Garden," on page 25.

Always an Exception

"Kate's Endless Stars" and "Star Garden," on pages 21 and 25 respectively, use a single fabric for the main stars and another for the secondary stars. This simple combination allows you to use either fabric for either type of star, and you don't have to decide which one goes where until after the units are cut.

Begin by arranging the units as initially planned; then flip them around to turn the main stars into secondary stars. Notice the change in the border stars and the quilt's center. Experimenting with the layout in this way illustrates the dramatic changes you can achieve by altering fabric positions—and you may discover you like the second arrangement better than the first!

Block detail of "Kate's Endless Stars"

OR

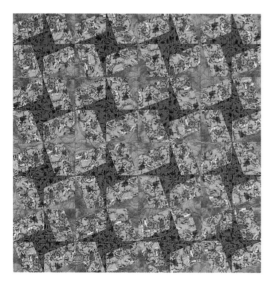

Block detail of "Star Garden"

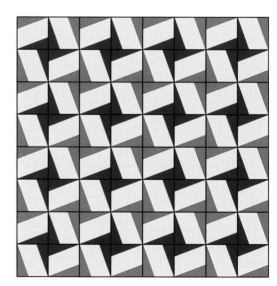

Reversing the positions of star units
changes the look of the quilt.

YOU'RE ABOUT TO DISCOVER one of the reasons Endless Stars are so much fun to make. Once you have the cutting technique mastered, your star units will quickly become rows of shining stars. Listed below are the supplies you will need to make these units, and directions for cutting them with a rotary cutter.

Tools and Supplies

To make the quilts in this book you will need the following supplies:

- A 4"- and a 6"-square ruler, each with ¼" markings in at least two opposite corners. Bias Square® rulers made by Martingale & Company work perfectly (www.martingale-pub.com).
- 6" x 24" rotary ruler
- Fabric Grips (to attach to rulers)
- Good quality sewing thread
- Rotary cutter with small blade
- Rotary-cutting mat (a revolving mat may work well for you but is optional)
- Sewing machine
- Super-fine silk pins (1¼" long)

STAR TIP

Apply Fabric Grips to the underside of your square ruler to keep it from slipping while you are cutting fabric. Place the grips in opposite corners near the ¼" mark. I use these sandpaper dots because they are easy to see, and they help me locate the ¼" lines quickly every time I cut.

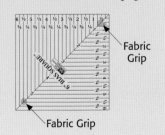

Fabric Grip

Fabric Grip

Cutting Endless Stars Units

Star units are cut from strip-pieced sets that usually contain three strips of fabric. Select your favorite project and make a test set; then return to these instructions to cut the star units.

The cutting instructions are the same for 4" and 6" square rulers. The directions for each project tell you which square ruler size to use.

1. Position the strip set on your cutting mat with the main-star fabric to the left.

STAR TIP

Keeping the main-star fabric on the left side when you cut star units is a good habit to get into. Some Endless Stars quilts have star units that contain multiple combinations of fabrics, such as "Shades of Summer" on page 42. It is easier to stay organized when you know the main-star fabric is always on the left.

2. Place the square ruler at the angle shown, tipping its top right edge downward.
3. Line up the ¼" mark on the upper-left corner of the ruler with the seam line between the main star fabric and background fabric. Make certain the entire ruler is on the strip set as shown.

4. Align the ¼" mark on the lower-right corner of the ruler with the seam line between the secondary star fabric and background fabric. Double-check to make sure the seam is aligned with the ¼" mark and not the ruler's corner.

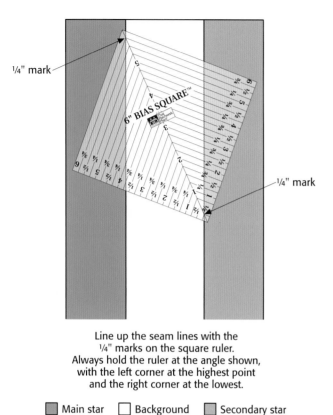

¼" mark

¼" mark

Line up the seam lines with the
¼" marks on the square ruler.
Always hold the ruler at the angle shown,
with the left corner at the highest point
and the right corner at the lowest.

■ Main star □ Background ■ Secondary star

5. Using a rotary cutter, carefully cut out the square to make one star unit.

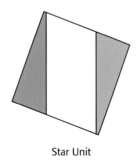

Star Unit

6. Look closely at your star unit. The ends of the seam lines should be a short distance away from the corners of the unit to accommodate the seam allowance when units are joined. If the seam lines emerge at the corners, the unit is not cut correctly.

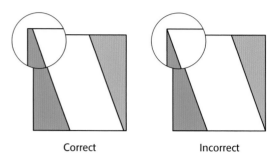

Correct   Incorrect

7. Use the same technique to cut additional star units from the remainder of the strip set, leaving a small amount of fabric between each unit. A 42"-long strip set will yield nine 4" star units or six 6" star units.

Handle the star units carefully, as their edges are cut on the fabrics' stretchy bias. There will be some waste at the end of each strip set.

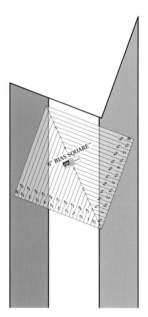

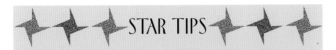

1. When cutting out the star units, it is helpful if you place your cutting mat on a corner of your cutting table so you can move around it easily as you cut out the unit.

2. Do not cut backwards or toward your body or non-cutting hand. Small (28 mm) rotary cutters are easiest to work with.

3. You may find it easier to hold the strip set horizontally as you cut rather than vertically as illustrated in this book. Do whatever makes you comfortable, making certain the ¼" marks are on the seam lines and you are using the rotary cutter correctly.

4. If you have a revolving cutting mat, place your strip set sideways on the mat and make your first cut so it cuts the excess strip set off, leaving you with only the fabric for one star unit on your mat. Rotate the mat to cut the unit.

5. Even if you choose not to mark the ¼" marks on your ruler with Fabric Grips, use one of the many products available to prevent your ruler from slipping.

6. Do not layer the strip sets and cut multiple star units at one time. This does not work, and the result will be inaccurate units.

7. A little practice goes a long way. After you've cut a few star units, you'll get a rhythm going.

Pressing Endless Stars

Bias edges are more prone to stretching than edges cut on a fabric's straight grain. Endless Stars units have bias edges on all four sides. Pressing, especially with steam or in a rough manner, can result in enough stretch to keep star units from matching up well with adjoining units. I recommend not pressing the units until they are sewn into complete rows. Star unit seams should be sharp and crisp if the strip sets were pressed thoroughly prior to cutting the units.

Once the units are sewn into rows, use a dry iron to lightly press the seam allowances carefully to one side. Press adjoining seam allowances in the next row in the opposite direction so the seams will butt together snugly when the rows are joined. If you have a seam that refuses to lie flat, turn the iron to steam and place it directly onto the seam without moving it back and forth.

When the quilt top is completed and sewn to its borders, use steam to press it carefully prior to layering. The small amount of pressing required to make an Endless Stars quilt should please everyone!

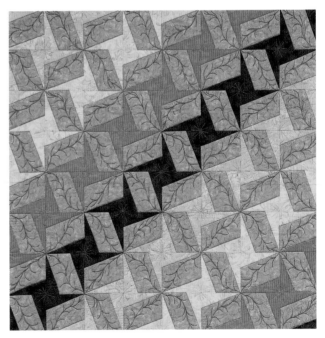

Careful pressing can help keep units from stretching, making it easier to match seams.

Creating Your Own Designs

THERE ARE A seemingly endless number of designs and variations for Endless Stars, and I hope you experiment to create your own layouts. Here are a few suggestions to assist you in the design process.

1. Photocopy Endless Stars diagram 1 or 2 and color in your Endless Stars design. Refer to "Quilt Elements" and "Endless Stars Patterns" on page 5.
2. Count the number of star units used for each color combination.
3. Double-check your figures by adding together the number of star units each type of star required; then compare that sum with the total number of star units in your design. The numbers should be the same.
4. Figure the number of strips you must cut to yield the correct number of star units from each color combination. Figure the yardage required for those strips based on the size of the star unit. The number of units you can cut per strip depends on the useable width of your fabrics and the size of the square ruler you use to cut the star units.

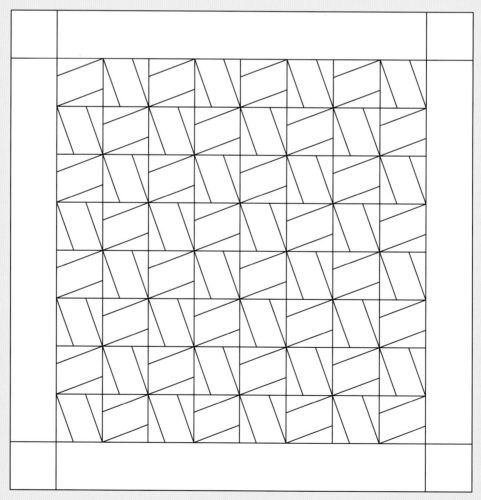

Endless Star Diagram 1

Designing with 4" Star Units

1. Cut the background strips 2½" wide and the star strips 2" wide.

2. A 4"-square ruler and 42"-long strip set yield nine units.

Designing with 6" Star Units

1. Cut the background strips 3¾" wide and the star strips 2½" wide.

2. A 6"-square ruler and 42"-long strip set yield six units.

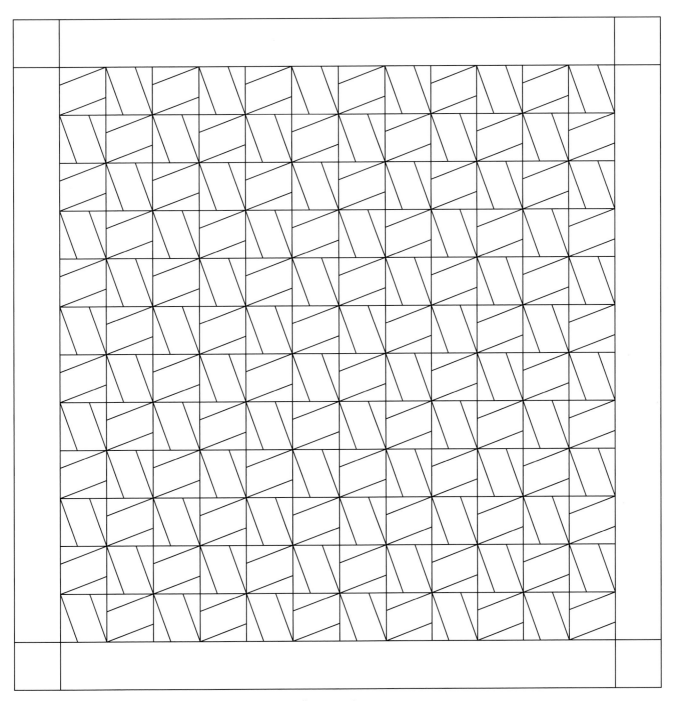

Endless Star Diagram 2

Assembling the Quilt Top

ONCE THE STAR UNITS are cut, Endless Stars quilts assemble quite quickly. Remember to handle the star units carefully to avoid stretching the bias edges. While I've rarely had problems with stretching, I've also taken extra care not to pull on the star units or press them unnecessarily.

Arranging Rows

If you're using more than two fabrics for your stars as in "Cool Confection" or "Summer Garden," I'd suggest laying out the star units in row order prior to sewing the rows together. A design wall or flannel yardage pinned to the wall works well for this. You'll want to avoid ripping out seams as doing so could stretch your star units.

Units are assembled in horizontal rows that are then pinned and stitched together to make the quilt top. Rarely do I use pins before this step. To assemble the rows I use the very fine silk pins mentioned in the supply list on page 9. These fine pins work especially well for any precision piecing and will hold the butted star-unit seams together tightly until they're stitched.

Adding Borders

The quilt's borders add another facet to its design. They frame the quilt with color while accenting the fabrics within. They also provide an area to display your quilting stitches and an opportunity to introduce another fabric into the quilt.

Yardage requirements for the projects in this book are for borders cut across the width of the fabric, from selvage to selvage. Most of the larger quilts have pieced borders, with the pieced seam centered at the quilt's midpoint. Yardage amounts increase when you cut long borders from directional fabric or along the lengthwise grain of the fabric.

The following methods for attaching borders helps the quilt lie flat, without rippled edges.

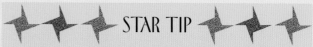

STAR TIP

Project instructions always include border yardage and cutting instructions, but sometimes it's fun to select your border fabrics after the star units are sewn together. Use a design wall to audition different fabrics already in your stash or take your pieced quilt top to the quilt shop and try out a variety of fabrics to see which look you like best.

Borders with Butted Corners

To attach borders with butted corners, follow these steps.

1. Measure the length of the quilt from top to bottom across its midpoint. Write down the measurement and mark the midpoint with a straight pin on each side of the quilt.

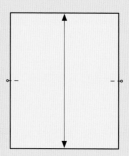

2. Referring to the pattern instructions for suggested widths, cut or piece two borders the exact length of your measurement.
3. Find the midpoint of each border strip and mark it with a pin. If the border is pieced from two 42"-long strips and you want the seam to be the midpoint of the border strip, divide the quilt's length in half and measure this distance from each side of the center seam. Check your measurements before cutting, and then trim the border strip.

4. Match the pin-marked midpoint on one side of the quilt to the midpoint of a border, pinning the two right sides together at that spot. Match and pin the ends of the border to the ends of the quilt. Match and pin the remaining length of the border to the side of the quilt, easing the quilt to fit the border if necessary.

Match midpoints and ends.

5. Sew the border to the quilt top with the border strip on top. Use the same method to attach a border to the opposite side of the quilt. Press seam allowances away from the quilt top.

6. Use the same technique to measure the quilt at its side-to-side midpoint, including the width of the side borders. Make two borders of that length and sew them to the ends of the quilt as you did the side borders. Press the seam allowances away from the quilt.

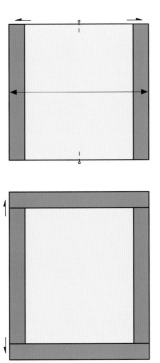

Borders with Corner Squares

Corner squares are an easy way to add another design element to the quilt. They can blend or contrast with the borders. Contrasting squares can be cut from a fabric already in the quilt or can be used to introduce something new. Corner squares are also helpful when you don't have enough fabric to cut four long borders.

1. Measure the lengths of both the horizontal and vertical midpoints of the quilt. Cut or piece two borders to match each measurement. Refer to the pattern instructions for suggested widths.

2. Attach side borders by following steps 3 through 5 of "Borders with Butted Corners" on page 14.

3. Cut four squares for border corners. The sides of each square should be the same length as the width of an unsewn border strip.

4. Sew a corner square to each end of the remaining border strips. Press the seam allowances toward the border strips.

5. Match and pin the midpoint of the border to the midpoint of the quilt top, right sides together. Match the corner square seams with the side border seams, butting seams together and pinning to secure. Match and pin the ends of each border to the ends of the quilt. Align the remaining length of the border to the quilt, easing the quilt if necessary to make it fit the border. Stitch together and press the seam allowance away from the quilt. Repeat to add the bottom border.

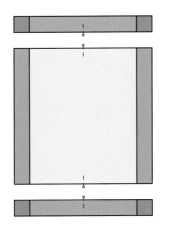
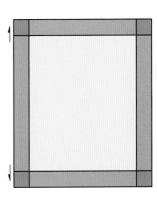

Borders with Mitered Corners

The term "mitered corners" refers to the 45° angle created where borders meet in each of the quilt's four corners. Mitered corners work especially well with directional or large-print fabrics and add a bit of elegance to the quilt.

1. Measure the quilt's length and width through its midpoints as described in step 1 of "Borders with Butted Corners" on page 14. Multiply the border width by two and add that length to each dimension. Finally, add 4" more to each of your totals. Your calculation should look like this: length (or width) of quilt + 2 x width of border + 4" = length of cut strip. Cut or piece two border strips to match each length.

2. Pin mark the midpoint of each border. Divide each of the quilt's midpoint measurements by two and pin mark that distance on either side of each border's center mark.

3. Match and pin the midpoint of a border to the midpoint along the corresponding side of the quilt, right sides together. Match and pin the marked ends to the two ends of that side of the quilt. Match and pin the remaining edges of the border to the entire side of the quilt, easing the quilt to fit the border if necessary.

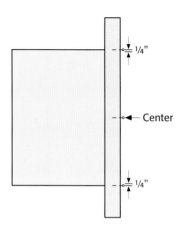

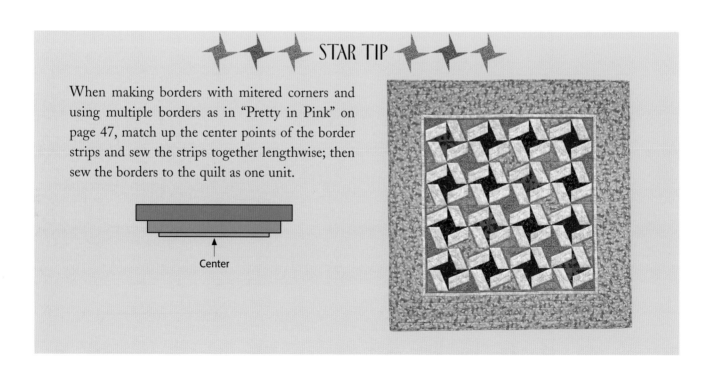

STAR TIP

When making borders with mitered corners and using multiple borders as in "Pretty in Pink" on page 47, match up the center points of the border strips and sew the strips together lengthwise; then sew the borders to the quilt as one unit.

Center

4. Stitch the border to the quilt top with the border strip on top, beginning and ending the seam ¼" from the end of the quilt. Backstitch at the beginning and end of the seam. Do not trim the excess fabric, because it will be needed to miter the corners. Repeat for the remaining border strips.

5. Working on a flat surface, place one end of the quilt's top border strip over the corresponding side border strip. Turn the top border strip under at a 45° angle. Check the angle using a ruler marked with a 45° angle. Press to mark the seam line.

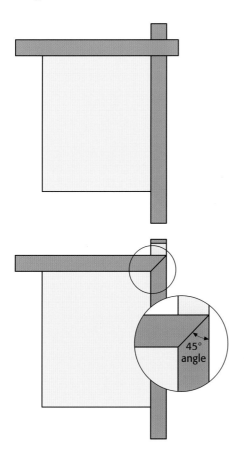

6. Fold the quilt right sides together and pin along the pressed line. Machine baste the pressed line and check the angle. If correct, stitch together, backstitching at the beginning and ending of the seam.

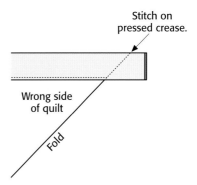

7. Trim away the excess fabric, leaving a ¼" seam allowance. Press. Repeat with the remaining corners.

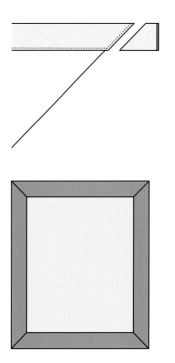

Finishing the Quilt

NOW THAT YOUR QUILT TOP is complete, consider its backing, the method of quilting you prefer to use (hand or machine), and the binding. Backing, though sometimes overlooked in the anticipation of finishing, is a visible layer and an important part of your quilt's design. Quilting stitches add a dimensional element to the finished quilt, and the binding can be used to frame the quilt one last time. Finishing your quilt nicely is as important as assembling the top correctly.

Quilt Backing

Don't hesitate to have fun with the back side of your quilt. There are many fabrics available to us that make beautiful backings. Large-scale florals, abstract patterns, and soft prints—the selection is endless. Consider a fabric you wouldn't normally use, or one that you just can't bring yourself to cut up into small pieces. My "Starshine" quilt is backed with a small monkey print reminiscent of Curious George. I just couldn't resist it, and it's definitely a surprise to find this fabric on the back of the quilt.

The yardage amount given with each project is enough to provide a pieced backing with a minimum of 4" of extra fabric on each side to allow for quilting. Larger quilts require two or three sections of fabric to piece a backing of the required size. Press the backing seams open to make hand quilting easier; for machine quilting, press to one side.

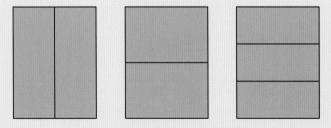

Common Backing Configurations

STAR TIP

Sometimes piecing the quilt back traditionally with 42" fabric and one or two seams results in considerable leftover backing fabric. This happens quite often with the larger project quilts in this book. Consider piecing your quilt's backing from leftover scraps or yardage from your fabric stash. A pieced back of multiple fabrics adds a bit of surprise and delight when it's turned over.

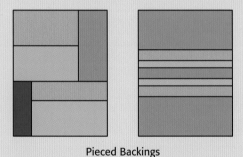

Pieced Backings

You can also purchase wider fabrics made especially for backings and enjoy a seam-free backing, while also avoiding a lot of leftover backing fabric.

Layering, Basting, and Quilting

Press the quilt top and backing carefully, making certain the seams lie flat. Cut away any loose threads. Open the batting and let the folds relax for a few hours or toss the batting into the dryer on fluff to remove the creases. Layer the backing, batting, and quilt top together. Baste and quilt as desired.

If you need more information regarding these steps, there are a number of excellent instruction books available, including *The Simple Joys of Quilting* by Joan Hanson and Mary Hickey, *Loving Stitches* by Jeana Kimball, and *Machine Quilting Made Easy* by Maurine Noble.

Attaching a Permanent Hanging Sleeve

One way to hang a quilt for display is to attach a permanent sleeve to its back prior to sewing the binding strips to the quilt.

1. Cut or piece a strip of fabric 8" wide and equal to the width of the quilt. Fold the short edges under by ½", toward the wrong side of the fabric and then fold under ½" again. Machine stitch to secure the folds. The sleeve should now be at least 2" shorter than the top edge of the quilt.

2. Fold the strip in half lengthwise, wrong sides together. Center the sleeve along the quilt's top edge and pin or baste the raw edges to the top edge of the quilt. The top of the sleeve will be secured when you attach the binding.

3. After you attach the binding, blindstitch the sleeve's bottom edge to the backing fabric, leaving a little fullness in the sleeve to accommodate the size of your hanging rod. Take care not to stitch through the top of the quilt.

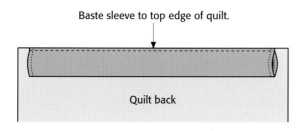

Baste sleeve to top edge of quilt.

Quilt back

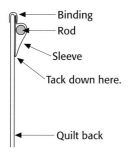

Binding
Rod
Sleeve
Tack down here.
Quilt back

Attaching a Temporary Hanging Sleeve

If you need a sleeve but do not want it to be permanent, add a sleeve after the quilt is bound.

Prepare a strip as directed in step 1 of "Attaching a Permanent Hanging Sleeve" at left. Fold the strip right sides together lengthwise and stitch along the sleeve's longest raw edge. Press the seam open.

Turn the sleeve right side out and press flat, centering the seam on one side. Center and pin the sleeve along the quilt's top edge. Blindstitch the sleeve securely just below the binding.

Make a little pleat to accommodate the hanging rod and blindstitch the bottom edge of the sleeve to the quilt's backing. Take care not to stitch through the top of the quilt.

Binding the Quilt

Double-fold bindings are made by sewing together fabric strips cut selvage to selvage along the crosswise grain. The projects in this book use binding strips cut 2" wide.

1. Hand or machine baste around the quilt, ⅛" to ¼" from the edge. Using a straight edge, trim the batting and backing even with the quilt edges. Be careful to keep the corners square. If desired, pin the hanging sleeve in place now.

2. Cut the number of binding strips required for your project. With right sides together, join strips end to end with diagonal seams to create one long strip. Trim the excess fabric from the seam allowances. Press the seam allowances open and trim away any little nubs that extend past the strip edges.

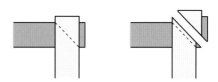

3. Fold the strip in half lengthwise, wrong sides together, and press. Turn under ¼" at a 45° angle at the beginning of the strip.

Fold line

4. Leaving a 4" tail at the beginning, place the binding along one side of the front of your quilt, raw edges matched. Check to make certain this placement won't make one of the binding's diagonal seams fall in a corner of the quilt.

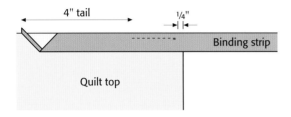

5. Sew the binding to the quilt with a ¼" seam allowance. Stop stitching ¼" from the end of the quilt and backstitch. Remove the quilt from the machine and cut the threads.

6. Fold the binding up and away from the quilt, creating a 45° angle with the fabric. Fold the strip back down, making certain the angle underneath remains intact. Reposition the quilt under the presser foot. Hold the strip in place and start stitching at the very edge of the quilt. Backstitch and continue. Repeat for all corners.

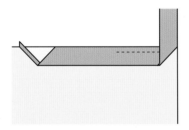

Fold binding up and away
from the quilt to create a 45° angle.

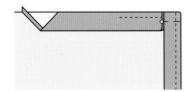

Fold binding even with quilt top,
keeping angle intact.

7. When you reach the beginning, stop sewing, overlap the beginning stitches by approximately 1", and cut away the excess binding. Trim the edge at a 45° angle and tuck the tail of the binding into the fold. Finish the seam.

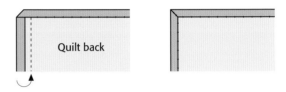

8. Fold the binding over the raw edges to the back of the quilt. Use a blind stitch to hand stitch the binding to the quilt back.

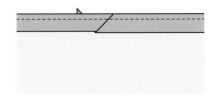

Labeling Your Quilt

As in the past, many of today's quilts will outlast their makers. Every quilt acquires its own history over time, and something as simple as a label will tell future generations about the origins of your quilt.

To record your quilt's information, use hand or machine embroidery, permanent fabric pens made specifically for quilters, or one of the popular computer techniques.

Your label should include at least the following information: the name of your quilt, your full name, where the quilt was made, its completion date, and, if the quilt was made for a specific person or reason, who it was made for or why it was made.

"Kate's Endless Stars" by Jean M. Potetz, 35½" x 35½", Granby, Connecticut.

SHADES OF LATE SUMMER herald the coming of fall. Brisk woodland walks with my dog Kate warm the cool evenings. For this three-fabric quilt, I based the color palette on my favorite sights of the season—Queen Anne's Lace drying to golden tan along the roadside, soft green moss bordering a shaded path, and the burgundy of ripening grapes.

Making this basic Endless Stars design will give you a good understanding of main and secondary stars. The pattern looks complex, but it is quite simple and goes together quickly. It also allows you to change its final appearance, even after the strips are sewn together and the star units are cut.

Fabric Guide

I chose the burgundy print for secondary stars because I wanted its large-scale floral to add emphasis to the border. Remember that secondary stars are also border stars, and when the same fabric is used for both, the border appears to extend into the quilt top. "Always an Exception," on page 8, offers suggestions to help you preview the layout before you sew the star units together.

Finished Quilt: 35½" x 35½" • Star Unit: 4"

Materials

Yardage is based on 42"-wide fabric.

- 1⅓ yards of burgundy for secondary stars and border
- ¾ yard of tan for background
- ⅔ yard of green for main stars
- 2⅔ yards for backing
- ⅓ yard for binding
- 40" x 40" piece of batting
- 4"-square ruler

If you want to select your border fabric after you have completed the star units, purchase ⅔ yard of burgundy fabric and ⅔ yard of border fabric.

Cutting

Cut all strips across the full width of the fabric (selvage to selvage). All measurements include ¼" seam allowances.

From the green fabric, cut:
− 8 strips, 2" x 42"

From the burgundy fabric, cut:
− 8 strips, 2" x 42"
− 4 strips, 4" x 42"; crosscut one 4" square from each strip

From the tan fabric, cut:
− 8 strips, 2½" x 42"

From the binding fabric, cut:
− 4 strips, 2" x 42"

Making the Star Units

1. Sew a 2" x 42" green (main star) strip to a 2½" x 42" tan (background) strip. Sew a 2" x 42" burgundy (secondary star) strip to the opposite side of the tan strip. Press seam allowances away from the center strip. Repeat to make 8 identical strip sets.

Make 8 strip sets.

2. Use a 4"-square ruler to cut 64 star units from the strip sets. Refer to "Cutting Endless Stars Units," on page 9 for detailed instructions. Handle the star units carefully, as their edges are cut on the fabric's stretchy bias.

Make 64 star units.

Assembling the Quilt Top

1. Arrange a horizontal star unit (main star down) to the left of a vertical star unit (main star left). Sew together along the edge where the main stars touch. Make a total of 32 identical horizontal-vertical star units. Do not press.

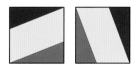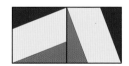

Make 32
horizontal-vertical star units.

2. Arrange two horizontal-vertical units side by side, placing the horizontal segment in each to the left. Sew the units together with secondary stars touching. Repeat to make a total of 16 identical pairs. Do not press.

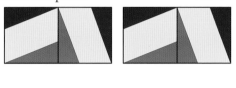

Make 16 horizontal-vertical pairs.

3. Place two horizontal-vertical pairs side by side, arranging each with a horizontal star unit on the left. Sew together to make one row. Repeat to make a total of eight rows. Do not press.

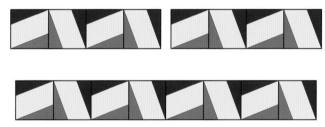

Make 8 rows.

4. Divide the rows into two groups of four rows each. Stack rows in one group with the main-star tips pointing up. Stack rows in the other group with the main-star tips pointing down.

5. Using a dry iron, press seam allowances in the direction indicated by the arrows in the diagram.

Main Stars pointing up

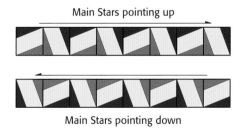

Main Stars pointing down

6. Pin and sew one row from each group together with main stars touching. Butt seams for a snug fit. Press the seam allowance toward the top row. Repeat to make a total of four identical units.

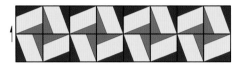

Two rows sewn together form main stars.
Make 4.

7. Pin and sew the four new units together with secondary stars touching. Butt seams for a snug fit. Press the seam allowances toward the top of the quilt as shown in the diagram.

Secondary stars emerge
when rows are sewn together.

8. Sew the 4" borders and corner squares to the quilt top. Refer to "Adding Borders" on page 14 and "Borders with Corner Squares" on page 15.

STAR TIP

I placed corner squares in the borders of "Kate's Endless Stars," and I chose to cut them from the same fabric as the borders. I like the added effect of a square in each corner of the quilt. It's a personal preference and adds a step to the quiltmaking process. "Borders with Butted Corners," described on page 14, would work just as well and save time, too.

Finishing the Quilt

Refer to "Finishing the Quilt" on page 18 for directions regarding the following steps.

1. Layer the quilt with batting and backing. Baste.
2. Quilt as desired. "Kate's Endless Stars" was machine quilted in a gentle, meandering pattern. The secondary stars are not quilted, so they stand out to shine on their own.
3. Attach a hanging sleeve if desired. Refer to page 19 for instructions.
4. Bind the quilt as described on page 19.
5. Label your quilt.

Quilt Diagram

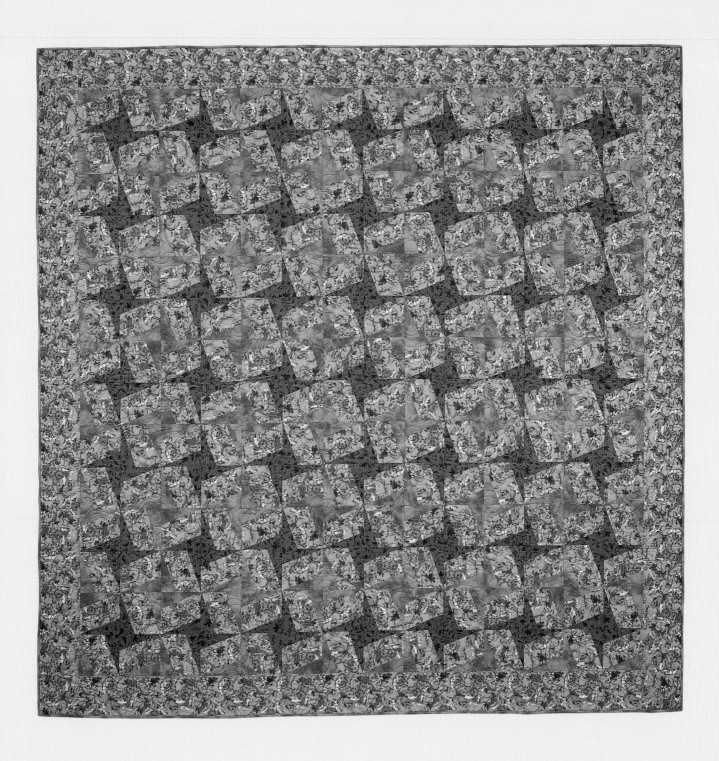

"Star Garden" by Jean M. Potetz, 88½" x 88½", Granby, Connecticut.
Machine quilted by Wilma Cogliantry.

THIS QUILT IS filled with the colors of spring — the deep purples of irises and tulips mixed with soft grass greens and touched by the golden tan of a meadowlark— shades that are most welcome after New England's winter whites. Six-inch star units make this large bed quilt go together quickly to brighten your day in record time.

Fabric Guide

When choosing which fabric will be used as the secondary star, remember this fabric will also become your border stars. I repeated the background fabric in the border and chose the subtle, softer transition of the marbleized green to the floral border rather than the brighter purple. This basic version of Endless Stars will give you a good understanding of main stars and secondary stars. Refer to "Which Fabric for Which Star?" on page 7 and "Always an Exception" on page 8 for ideas to help you customize this pattern.

Finished Quilt: 88½" x 88½" • **Star Unit:** 6"

Materials

Yardage is based on 42"-wide fabric.

- 6¼ yards of a large-scale floral for the background and border*
- 3¼ yards of purple for the main stars
- 3¼ yards of green for the secondary stars
- 8⅓ yards for the backing
- ⅔ yards for the binding
- 93" x 93" piece of batting
- 6"-square ruler

If you want to select your border fabric after you have completed the star units, purchase 4½ yards of large-scale floral fabric and 1¾ yards of border fabric.

Cutting

Cut all strips across the full width of the fabric (selvage to selvage). All measurements include ¼" seam allowances.

From the purple fabric, cut:
- 33 strips, 2½" x 42"

From the green fabric, cut:
- 33 strips, 2½" x 42"

From the large-scale floral, cut:
- 33 strips, 3¾" x 42"
- 9 strips, 6" x 42"; crosscut 4 squares from 1 strip

From the binding fabric, cut:
- 10 strips, 2" x 42"

Making the Star Units

1. Sew a 2½" x 42" purple (main star) strip to a 3¾" x 42" floral (background) strip. Sew a 2½" x 42" green (secondary star) strip to the opposite side of the floral strip. Press seam allowances away from the center strip. Repeat to make 33 identical strip sets.

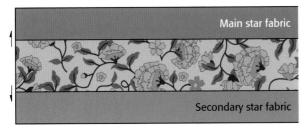

Main star fabric

Secondary star fabric

Make 33 strip sets.

STAR TIP

If you cannot cut six star units from each strip set, you will need to cut additional fabric strips to make the number of star units required. Cut seven additional strips from each star and background fabric to make a total of 40 strip sets. Yardage requirements allow for these extra strips.

2. Use a 6"-square ruler to cut 196 star units from the strip sets. Refer to "Cutting Endless Stars Units" on page 9 for detailed instructions. Handle the star units carefully, as their edges are cut on the fabric's stretchy bias.

Cut 196 star units.

Assembling the Quilt Top

1. Arrange a horizontal star unit (main star down) to the left of a vertical star unit (main star left). Sew together along the edge where the main star units touch. Repeat to make a total of 98 identical horizontal-vertical star units. Do not press.

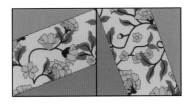

Make 98
horizontal-vertical star units.

2. Divide the horizontal-vertical units into fourteen sets of seven units each.
3. Arrange a set of seven horizontal-vertical units into a row, placing the horizontal star units to the left. Sew the units together with secondary stars touching. Make 14 rows. Do not press.

Make 14 rows.

4. Divide the rows into two groups, each containing seven rows. Stack rows in one group with main-star tips pointing up. Stack rows in the second group with main-star tips pointing down. Using a dry

iron, press seam allowances in each group in the direction indicated by the arrows in the diagram.

Main Stars pointing up

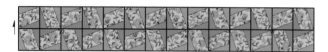

Main Stars pointing down

5. Select one row from each group. Pin and sew together along main stars, butting seams for a snug fit. Press the seam allowance toward the top row. Repeat to make a total of seven identical units.

Two rows sewn together form main stars.
Make 7.

6. Pin and sew the seven new units together to complete the quilt top. Press the seam allowances toward the top of the quilt as shown in the diagram.

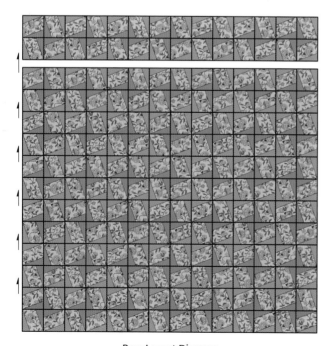

Row Layout Diagram

7. Sew the 6" border strips and corner squares to the quilt top. Refer to "Adding Borders" on page 14 and "Borders with Corner Squares" on page 15.

Finishing the Quilt

Refer to "Finishing the Quilt" on page 18 for directions regarding the following steps.

1. Layer the quilt with batting and backing. Baste.
2. Quilt as desired. "Star Garden" was machine quilted using a beautiful swirling pattern that reminds me of a summer breeze.
3. Bind the quilt as described on page 19.
4. Label your quilt.

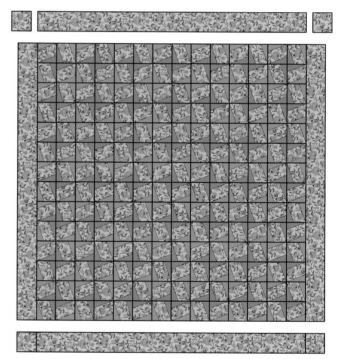

Quilt Diagram

New England Asters

"New England Asters" by Jean M. Potetz, 44½" x 55½",
Granby, Connecticut. Machine quilted by Wilma Cogliantry.

 IN THE FALL of each year, dark purple asters dot the New England roadsides. Mixed among the goldenrod, they add sparkle to the landscape. Reminiscent of traditionally pieced two-color quilts, this project goes together easily, with delightful results. The most difficult part of choosing material for this quilt is bringing home only two fabrics from the quilt shop!

Fabric Guide

Almost any two-color combination will work well for this quilt as long as it provides good contrast. Refer to "Endless Stars Fabrics" on page 7 for more fabric selection tips.

Finished Quilt: 44½" x 55½" • Star Unit: 6"

Materials

Yardage is based on 42"-wide fabric.

- 3 yards of purple for the stars and border*
- 1⅓ yards of a light, airy print for the background
- 3¼ yards for the backing
- ½ yard for the binding
- 49" x 60" piece of batting
- 6"-square ruler

If you want to select your border fabric after you have completed the star units, purchase 1⅔ yards of purple fabric and 1¼ yards of border fabric.

Cutting

Cut all strips across the full width of the fabric (selvage to selvage). All measurements include ¼" seam allowances.

From the purple fabric, cut:
– 16 strips, 2½" x 42"
– 6 strips, 6" x 42"

From the light, airy print, cut:
– 8 strips, 3¾" x 42"

From the binding fabric, cut:
– 6 strips, 2" x 42"

STAR TIP

Make your quilt smaller or larger by using the cutting directions for "Kate's Endless Stars" or "Star Garden," cutting both the main and secondary star strips from just one fabric.

Making the Star Units

1. Sew a 2½" x 42" purple (star) strip to a 3¾" x 42" airy print (background) strip. Sew a 2½" x 42" purple strip to the opposite side of the print strip. Repeat to make eight identical strip sets. Press seam allowances away from the center strip.

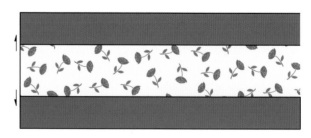

Make 8 strip sets.

STAR TIP

If you cannot cut six star units from each strip set, you will need to cut additional fabric strips to make the number of star units required. Cut four additional star strips and two additional background strips to make a total of 10 strip sets. Yardage requirements allow for these extra strips.

2. Use a 6"-square ruler to cut 48 star units from the strip sets. Refer to "Cutting Endless Stars Units" on page 9 for detailed instructions. Handle the star units carefully, as their edges are cut on the fabric's stretchy bias.

Cut 48 star units.

Assembling the Quilt Top

1. Place a horizontal star unit to the left of a vertical star unit. Sew together. Repeat to make a total of 24 identical horizontal-vertical units. Do not press.

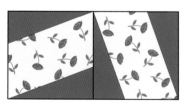

Make 24
horizontal-vertical star units.

2. Divide the horizontal-vertical units into eight groups of three units each.

3. Arrange one group into a row, placing the horizontal star units to the left. Sew together. Repeat to make a total of eight rows. Do not press.

Make 8 rows.

4. Divide the rows into two groups, each containing four rows. Stack rows in one group with a horizontal star unit to the left. Stack rows in the second group with a vertical star unit to the left. Using a dry iron, press seam allowances in each group in the direction indicated by the arrows in the diagram.

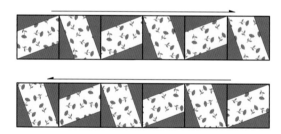

5. Select one row from each group. Pin and sew together, butting seams for a snug fit. Press the seam allowance toward the top row. Repeat to make a total of four identical units.

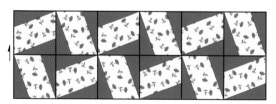

Make 4.

6. Pin and sew the four new units together. Press the seam allowances toward the top of the quilt as shown in the diagram.

Row Layout Diagram

7. Sew the 6" border strips to the quilt top following the directions for "Borders with Butted Corners" on page 14. Attach the top and bottom border strips before you attach the side borders.

Finishing the Quilt

Refer to "Finishing the Quilt" on page 18 for directions regarding the following steps.

1. Layer the quilt with batting and backing. Baste.
2. Quilt as desired. "New England Asters" was machine-quilted in a swirling star pattern that reinforces the quilt's light and airy appearance.
3. Bind the quilt as described on page 19.
4. Label your quilt.

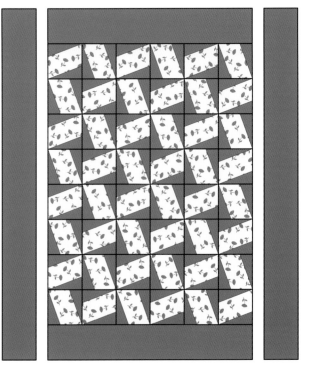

Quilt Diagram

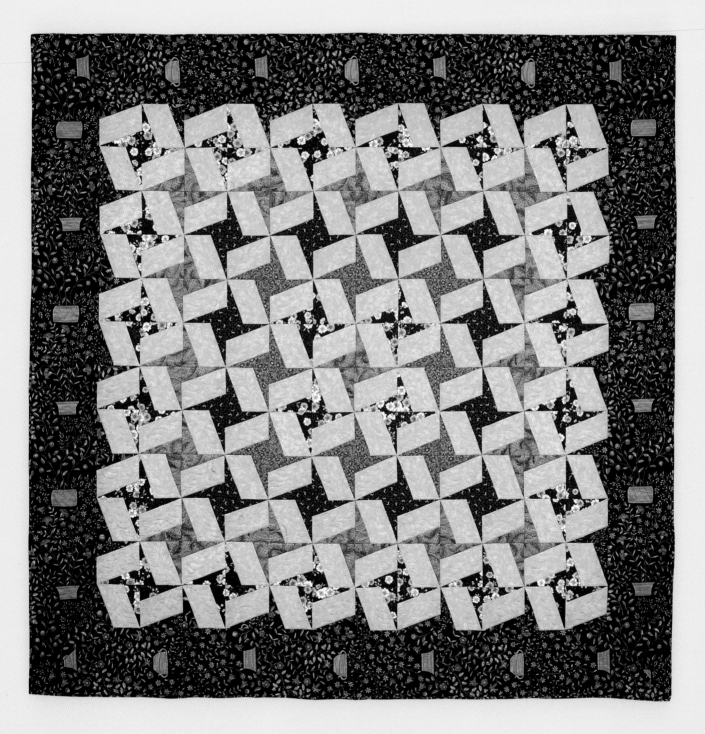

"Summer Nights" by Jean M. Potetz, 83½" x 83½", Granby, Connecticut.
Machine quilted by Wilma Cogliantry.

STARRY SKIES, golden moonlight, and cool breezes filled with the fragrance of wildflowers and soft green grasses—perfect summer nights. In the tradition of medallion quilts, this design radiates from its center outward. While the quilt appears to be assembled by adding multiple borders around a center square, it is actually constructed by sewing together horizontal rows.

Fabric Guide

The subtle shadings of the marbleized gold background added just a hint of texture and worked perfectly to tie together the varied scales and colors of fabrics used in the main and secondary stars. Refer to "Endless Stars Fabrics" on page 7 for tips that will help you select fabrics for your quilt.

Finished Quilt: 77½" x 77½" • **Star Unit:** 6"

Materials

Yardage is based on 42"-wide fabric.

- 1⅔ yards of purple print for star 1
- 1¼ yards of green print for star 2 (center star)
- 1 yard of black-and-tan print for star 3
- ¾ yard of blue print for star 4
- 2⅔ yards of a large-scale navy print for star 5 (border stars) and borders. Directional prints may require extra yardage when used in borders.*
- 3½ yards of marbleized gold for the background
- 7½ yards for the backing
- ⅔ yard for the binding
- 82" x 82" piece of batting
- 6"-square ruler

If you want to select your border fabric after you have completed the star units, purchase 1 yard of large-scale navy print and 1⅔ yards of border fabric.

Cutting

Cut all strips across the full width of the fabric (selvage to selvage). All measurements include ¼" seam allowances.

From the purple print, cut:
– 17 strips, 2½" x 42"

From the green print, cut:
– 12 strips, 2½" x 42"

From the black-and-tan print, cut:
– 9 strips 2½" x 42"

From the blue print, cut:
– 6 strips 2½" x 42"

From the large-scale navy print, cut:
– 8 strips, 2½" x 42"
– 8 strips, 6" x 42"

From the gold background fabric, cut:
– 26 strips 3¾" x 42"

From the binding fabric, cut:
– 9 strips, 2" x 42"

Making the Star Units

1. Referring to the materials list on page 34, make a number label for each fabric and attach it to a small swatch of each.

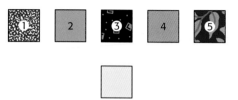

Background

STAR TIP

If you cannot cut six star units from each strip set, you will need to cut additional fabric strips to make the number of star units required. You will need one more strip set each of fabrics 1 and 2, 1 and 4, 1 and 5, and 3 and 2. To make these strip sets, cut the required strips of star fabric and four additional background strips. Yardage requirements allow for these extra strips.

2. Referring to the strip-set diagrams on this page, sew the 2½" star strips to the 3¾" background strips. Press seam allowances away from the center strips.

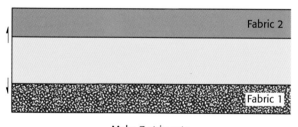

Make 7 strip sets.

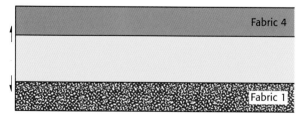

Make 2 strip sets.

Make 8 strip sets.

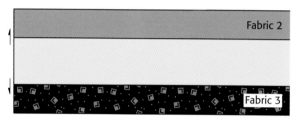

Make 5 strip sets.

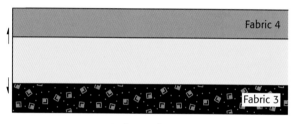

Make 4 strip sets.

3. Use a 6"-square ruler to cut the number of star units required from each strip set as shown. Refer to "Cutting Endless Stars Units" on page 9 for detailed instructions. Handle the star units carefully, as their edges are cut on the fabric's stretchy bias.

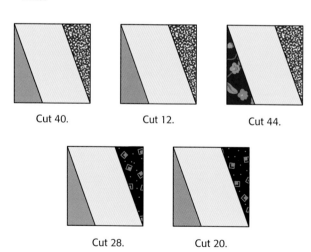

Cut 40.   Cut 12.   Cut 44.

Cut 28.   Cut 20.

Assembling the Quilt Top

1. Referring to the row layout diagram below, arrange the star units into 12 horizontal rows.
2. Sew the units in each row together, always sewing like star fabrics together. Use a dry iron to press seams in adjoining rows in opposite directions as illustrated by the pressing arrows in the row layout diagram.

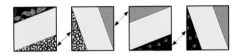

Always sew like star fabrics together.

Row Layout Diagram

3. Butting seams, pin and sew the rows together. Use a dry iron to press seam allowances toward the top of the quilt.
4. Sew the borders to the quilt top following the directions for "Borders with Mitered Corners" on page 16.

Finishing the Quilt

Refer to "Finishing the Quilt" on page 18 for directions regarding the following steps.

1. Layer the quilt with batting and backing. Baste.
2. Quilt as desired. "Starshine" was machine quilted with a beautiful feather and vine pattern that surrounds the stars.
3. Bind the quilt as described on page 19.
4. Label your quilt.

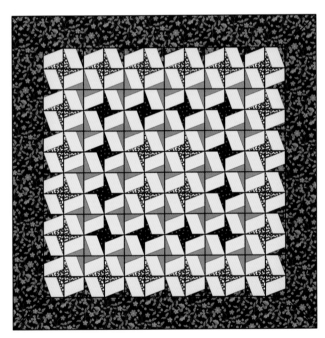

Quilt Diagram

 1   2   3   4   5

Background

Summer Garden

"Zinnia Patch " by Jean M. Potetz, 55½" x 66½", Granby, Connecticut.
Machine quilted by Wilma Cogliantry.

I HAVE ALWAYS loved zinnias. It's amazing to me that one packet of mixed seeds can create so many joyful color combinations. Placing the flowers in a jar on my old oak table brings their colors inside during the summer, but this quilt captures their brilliant shades for you to enjoy during the gray days of winter. I think you'll find that "Summer Garden" is a fun quilt that lends itself well to experimentation with fabric and color.

Fabric Guide

I chose a bold green fabric with subtle texture for the quilt's background. My stars are sewn from almost-solid prints in bright, vibrant shades of color reminiscent of the zinnias in my garden. Try gathering your palette from the colors used by Mother Nature—she's *never* wrong.

However, if these brights seem too bold to you, consider a light, airy floral for the background. Choose textured, solid fabrics from the colors found in the background's floral for your stars. Use the floral in the border as well. Your quilt will still sparkle—just not as brightly.

Finished Quilt: 55½" x 66½" • **Star Unit:** 6"

Materials

Yardage is based on 42"-wide fabric.

- 2¼ yards of green for background
- 1¼ yards of pink batik for borders
- 1 yard of pink for star 1
- ¾ yard of yellow for star 2
- ¾ yard of orange for star 3
- 1 yard of purple for star 4
- 3⅔ yards for backing
- ½ yard for binding
- 60" x 71" piece of batting
- 6"-square ruler

Cutting

Cut all strips across the full width of the fabric (selvage to selvage). All measurements include ¼" seam allowances.

From the pink fabric, cut:
– 8 strips, 2½" x 42"

From the yellow fabric, cut:
– 8 strips, 2½" x 42"

From the orange fabric, cut:
– 8 strips, 2½" x 42"

From the purple fabric, cut:
– 8 strips, 2½" x 42"

From the green fabric, cut:
– 16 strips, 3¾" x 42"

From the pink batik, cut:
– 8 strips, 6" x 42"

From the binding fabric, cut:
– 7 strips, 2" x 42"

Making the Star Units

1. Referring to the materials list on page 38, make a number label for each fabric and attach it to a small swatch of each.

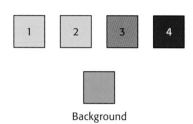

Background

✦✦✦ STAR TIP ✦✦✦

If you cannot cut six star units from each strip set, you will need to cut additional fabric strips in order to make the necessary number of star units. You will need one more strip set of fabrics 1 and 1, and of 4 and 4. To make these strip sets, cut the star-fabric strips required and two additional background strips. Yardage requirements allow for these extra strips.

2. Referring to the strip-set diagram below, sew the 2½" star strips to the 3¾" background strips. Press seam allowances away from the center background strips.

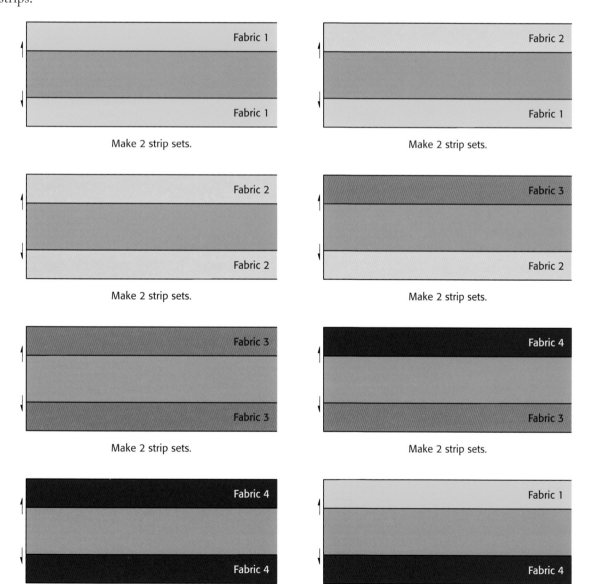

Fabric 1 / Fabric 1
Make 2 strip sets.

Fabric 2 / Fabric 1
Make 2 strip sets.

Fabric 2 / Fabric 2
Make 2 strip sets.

Fabric 3 / Fabric 2
Make 2 strip sets.

Fabric 3 / Fabric 3
Make 2 strip sets.

Fabric 4 / Fabric 3
Make 2 strip sets.

Fabric 4 / Fabric 4
Make 2 strip sets.

Fabric 1 / Fabric 4
Make 2 strip sets.

3. Use a 6"-square ruler to cut the number of star units required from each strip set, as shown. Refer to "Cutting Endless Stars Units" on page 9 for detailed instructions. Handle the star units carefully, as their edges are cut on the fabric's stretchy bias.

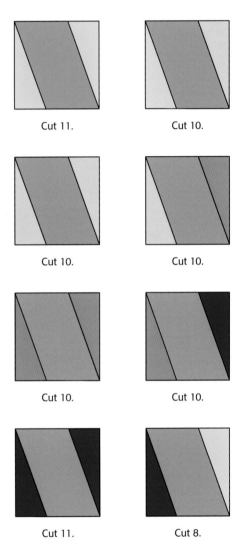

Cut 11.   Cut 10.

Cut 10.   Cut 10.

Cut 10.   Cut 10.

Cut 11.   Cut 8.

Assembling the Quilt Top

1. Arrange the star units into 10 horizontal rows as shown in the row layout diagram below. Each row contains eight star units.
2. Sew the units in each row together, always sewing like star fabrics together. Use a dry iron to press seams in adjoining rows in opposite directions as illustrated by the pressing arrows.

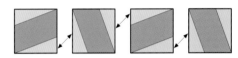

Always sew like star fabrics together.

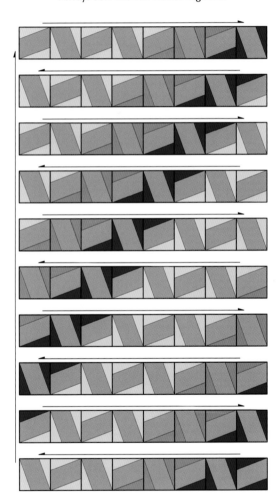

Row Layout Diagram

3. Butting seams, pin and sew the rows together. Use a dry iron to press seam allowances toward the top of the quilt.

4. Sew the 6" borders to the quilt top following the directions for "Borders with Butted Corners" on page 14. Attach the top and bottom borders first.

Finishing the Quilt

Refer to "Finishing the Quilt" on page 18 for directions regarding the following steps.

1. Layer the quilt with batting and backing. Baste.

2. Quilt as desired. My quilt was machine quilted to make the stars appear to be rows of zinnias with their centers stitched with multicolored thread. Zinnia stems are quilted into the background.

3. Bind the quilt as described on page 19.

4. Label your quilt.

Quilt Diagram

Background

Cool Confection

"Shades of Summer" by Jean M. Potetz, 43" x 43", Granby, Connecticut.
Machine quilted by Wilma Cogliantry.

A FABRIC GARDEN filled with cool shades of summer flowers—petunias and marigolds, daisies and morning glories—this quilt fills my house with blooms all year long. You'll definitely have fun putting this project together. Its scrappy mixture of colors and textures creates a lot of excitement within its sixteen little stars.

Fabric Guide

When I make a scrap quilt, I like to divide my fabrics into groups by color, value, texture, and scale. Looking at the quilt diagram on page 46, notice that the main stars (1, 2, and 3) are bright, multicolored, medium-scale prints. Stars 1 and 2 are also corner stars, so I placed my brightest fabrics there for balance. The secondary stars (4, 5, and 6) are bright tone-on-tone prints of small to medium scales. Since star 4 is the center star, I chose my most vivid tone-on-tone fabric to make it emerge, and to balance it with the bright corners. For more ideas about positioning your fabrics, refer to "Which Fabric for Which Star?" on page 7.

Finished Quilt: 43" x 43" • **Star Unit:** 4"

Materials

Yardage is based on 42"-wide fabric.

- 1⅔ yards of purple print for (main) star 1 and the border*
- 1 yard of light print for the background
- ⅜ yard of gold-and-purple print for (main) star 2
- ⅜ yard of green print for (main) star 3
- ⅜ yard of bright pink print for (secondary) star 4
- ⅜ yard of light pink print for (secondary) star 5
- ⅜ yard of gold print for (secondary) star 6
- 3 yards for the backing
- ⅜ yard for the binding
- 47" x 47" piece of batting
- 4"-square ruler

If you want to select your border fabric after you have completed the star units, purchase ⅜ yard of purple print and 1¼ yards of border fabric.

Cutting

Cut all strips across the full width of the fabric (selvage to selvage). All measurements include ¼" seam allowances.

From the purple print, cut:
- 3 strips, 2" x 42"
- 4 strips, 7½" x 42"; crosscut a 7½" square from each strip

From the gold-and-purple print, cut:
- 3 strips, 2" x 42"

From the green print, cut:
- 3 strips, 2" x 42"

From the bright pink print, cut:
- 3 strips, 2" x 42"

From the light pink print, cut:
- 3 strips, 2" x 42"

From the gold print, cut:
- 3 strips, 2" x 42"

From the light print, cut:
- 9 strips, 2½" x 42"

From the binding fabric, cut:
- 5 strips, 2" x 42"

Making the Star Units

1. Referring to the materials list on page 43, make a number label for each fabric and attach it to a small swatch of each. Main stars are numbers 1, 2, and 3; secondary stars are numbers 4, 5, and 6.

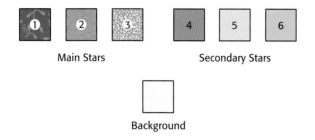

Main Stars   Secondary Stars

Background

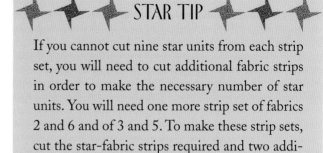

STAR TIP

If you cannot cut nine star units from each strip set, you will need to cut additional fabric strips in order to make the necessary number of star units. You will need one more strip set of fabrics 2 and 6 and of 3 and 5. To make these strip sets, cut the star-fabric strips required and two additional background strips. Yardage requirements allow for these extra strips.

2. Referring to the strip-set diagram below, sew the 2" star strips to the 2½" background strips. Press seam allowances away from the center background strips.

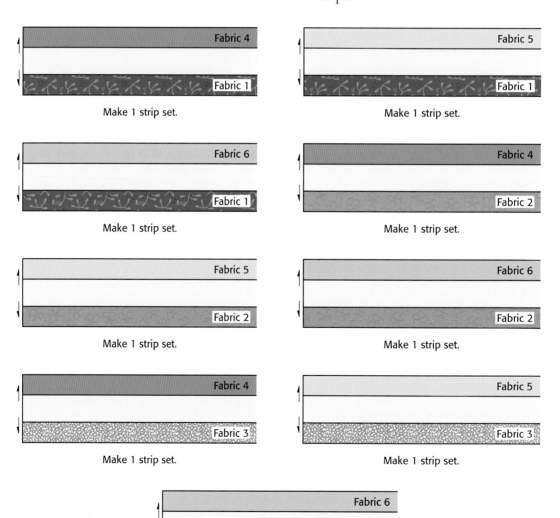

Fabric 4 / Fabric 1 Make 1 strip set.	Fabric 5 / Fabric 1 Make 1 strip set.
Fabric 6 / Fabric 1 Make 1 strip set.	Fabric 4 / Fabric 2 Make 1 strip set.
Fabric 5 / Fabric 2 Make 1 strip set.	Fabric 6 / Fabric 2 Make 1 strip set.
Fabric 4 / Fabric 3 Make 1 strip set.	Fabric 5 / Fabric 3 Make 1 strip set.

Fabric 6 / Fabric 3

Make 1 strip set.

3. Use a 4"-square ruler to cut the number of star units required from each strip set as shown in the diagram below. Refer to "Cutting Endless Stars Units" on page 9 for detailed instructions. Handle the star units carefully, as their edges are cut on the fabric's stretchy bias.

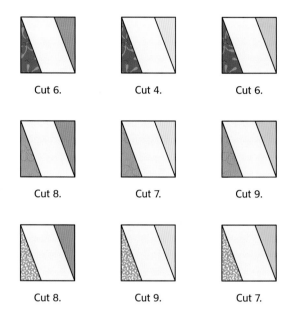

Cut 6.   Cut 4.   Cut 6.

Cut 8.   Cut 7.   Cut 9.

Cut 8.   Cut 9.   Cut 7.

Assembling the Quilt Top

1. Referring to the row layout diagram at right, arrange the star units into eight horizontal rows. Each row contains eight star units.
2. Sew the units in each row together, always sewing like fabric to like fabric. Use a dry iron to press seams in adjoining rows in opposite directions as illustrated by the pressing arrows.

Always sew like star fabrics together.

Row Layout Diagram

3. Butting seams, pin and sew the rows together. Use a dry iron to press seam allowances toward the top of the quilt.
4. Sew the 7½" borders and corner squares to the quilt top following the directions for "Borders with Corner Squares" on page 15.

Finishing the Quilt

Refer to "Finishing the Quilt" on page 18 for directions regarding the following steps.

1. Layer the quilt with batting and backing. Baste.

2. Quilt as desired. "Cool Confection" was machine quilted. A soft, feather-like design was used in each individual background piece and repeated in a larger scale in the border. The individual stars are outlined with a straight stitch.

3. If desired, attach a hanging sleeve as described on page 19.

4. Bind the quilt as described on page 19.

5. Label your quilt.

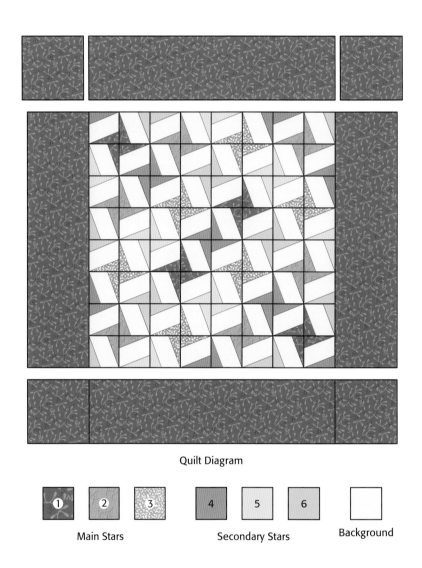

Quilt Diagram

Main Stars   Secondary Stars   Background

"Softly Spring" by Jean M. Potetz, 42" x 42", Granby, Connecticut.
Machine quilted by Wilma Cogliantry.

 THE COMBINATION OF delicate pinks, marbled creams, and varied greens in this quilt reminds me of a bouquet full of spice-scented carnations, lily of the valley, and gentle spring foliage. A variation of "Cool Confection," this quilt offers an added dimension—accent strips that surround each secondary star. The technique is an easy one and can be adapted for use with any Endless Stars pattern.

Fabric Guide

As shown in the quilt diagram on page 51, the quilt's main stars (1, 2, and 3) are dark shades of green and wine; the fabrics are similar in scale, texture, and value. The secondary stars (4, 5, and 6) are sewn from small-scale pink prints in lighter shades, the brightest of which I used for the quilt's center star (4). The soft green accent strip surrounding each secondary star is also used as the inner border and separates the cream background from the middle border of the same color. For ideas to help you select fabrics, refer to "Endless Stars Fabrics" on page 7 and "Which Fabric for Which Star?" on page 7.

Finished Quilt: 42" x 42" • Star Unit: 4"

Materials

Yardage is based on 42"-wide fabric.

- 1¼ yards of cream for the background and middle border*
- 1⅝ yards of pink-and-tan print for (secondary) star 5, outer border, and binding*
- ⅔ yard of soft green for the background accent strip and inner border*
- ⅜ yard of medium green print for (main) star 1
- ⅜ yard of wine print for (main) star 2
- ⅜ yard of dark green print for (main) star 3
- ⅜ yard of dark pink print for (secondary) star 4
- ⅜ yard of medium pink print for (secondary) star 6
- 3 yards for the backing
- 46" x 46" piece of batting
- 4"-square ruler

If you want to select your border fabrics after you have completed the star units, purchase 1 yard of cream fabric, ⅜ yard of pink-and-tan print, and ⅓ yard of soft green fabric. You will need ¼ yard of inner-border fabric, ¼ yard of middle-border fabric, 1 yard of outer-border fabric, and ⅜ yard of binding fabric.

Cutting

Cut all strips across the full width of the fabric (selvage to selvage). All measurements include ¼" seam allowances.

From the medium green print, cut:
− 3 strips, 2" x 42"

From the wine print, cut:
− 3 strips, 2" x 42"

From the dark green print, cut:
− 3 strips, 2" x 42"

From the dark pink print, cut:
− 3 strips, 2" x 42"

From the pink-and-tan print, cut:
− 8 strips, 2" x 42"
− 4 strips, 6" x 42"

From the medium pink print, cut:
− 3 strips, 2" x 42"

From the soft green accent fabric, cut:
− 13 strips, ¾" x 42"

From the cream fabric, cut:
− 9 strips, 2¼" x 42"
− 4 strips, 1¼" x 42"

Making the Star Units

1. Referring to the materials list on page 48, make a number label for each fabric and attach it to a small swatch of each. Main stars are numbers 1, 2, and 3; secondary stars are numbers 4, 5, and 6. Label the background and accent fabrics if you wish.

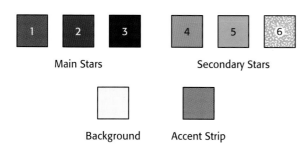

Main Stars   Secondary Stars

Background   Accent Strip

2. Sew a ¾"-wide accent strip to a 2¼"-wide background strip. Press the seam allowance toward the wider background strip. Repeat to make nine identical strip sets.

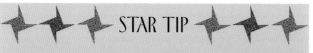

Make 9 strip sets.

3. Referring to the strip-set diagram at right, sew the 2" main-star strips to the background portion of the strip sets. Complete the strip sets by sewing the secondary-star strips to the accent fabric. Press seam allowances away from the center background strips.

STAR TIP

If you cannot cut nine star units from each strip set, you will need to cut additional fabric strips in order to make the necessary number of star units. You will need one more strip set of fabrics 2 and 6 and of 3 and 5. To make these strip sets, cut the star-fabric strips required and two additional background and accent border strips. Yardage requirements allow for these extra strips.

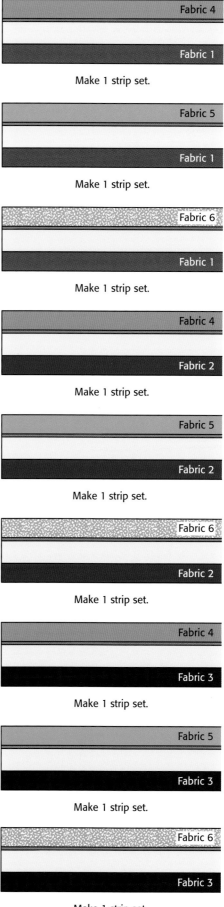

Make 1 strip set.

Make 1 strip set.

Make 1 strip set.

Make 1 strip set.

Make 1 strip set.

Make 1 strip set.

Make 1 strip set.

Make 1 strip set.

Make 1 strip set.

4. To cut the star units, place the bottom right corner of the 4" ruler's ¼" mark on the seam line of the accent strip and the secondary-star strip. Refer to "Cutting Endless Stars Units" on page 9 for additional cutting instructions. Cut the number of star units required from each fabric combination, as shown. Handle the star units carefully, as their edges are cut on the fabric's bias.

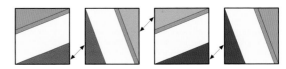

Place ¼" mark on square ruler on the seam line of the secondary star strip and the accent strip.

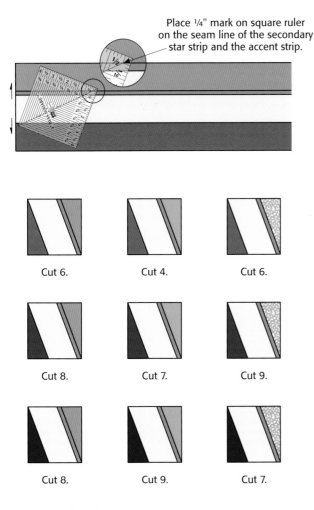

Cut 6.　　Cut 4.　　Cut 6.

Cut 8.　　Cut 7.　　Cut 9.

Cut 8.　　Cut 9.　　Cut 7.

⭑ ⭑ ⭑ STAR TIP ⭑ ⭑ ⭑

Accented backgrounds can be used in any of the quilts in this book. In "Pretty in Pink," only the secondary stars are outlined. However, a background can be made of any combination of fabric strips as long as its total width matches the width listed in the project's cutting instructions.

Assembling the Quilt Top

1. Arrange the star units into eight horizontal rows as shown in the row layout diagram below. Each row contains eight star units.
2. Sew the units in each row together, always sewing like star fabrics together. Use a dry iron to press seams in adjoining rows in opposite directions as illustrated by the pressing arrows.

Always sew like star fabrics together.

Row Layout Diagram

3. Butting seams, pin and sew the rows together. Use a dry iron to press seam allowances toward the top of the quilt.

4. Sew one inner-, one middle-, and one outer-border strip together in order. Press the seam allowances toward the outer-border strip. Repeat to make a total of four border strips.

5. Sew the borders to the quilt top following the directions on page 16 for "Borders with Mitered Corners."

Finishing the Quilt

Refer to "Finishing the Quilt" on page 18 for directions regarding the following steps.

1. Layer the quilt with batting and backing. Baste.

2. Quilt as desired. "Pretty in Pink" was machine quilted with circles in each outlined star. The border is quilted with straight lines to frame the quilt.

3. Attach a hanging sleeve as described on page 19.

4. Bind the quilt as described on page 19.

5. Label your quilt.

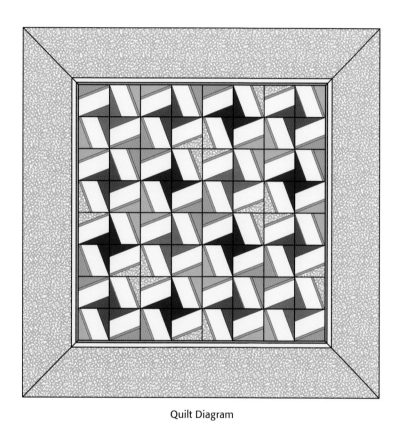

Quilt Diagram

1	2	3		4	5	6

Main Stars   Secondary Stars

Background   Accent Strip

Sean's Stars

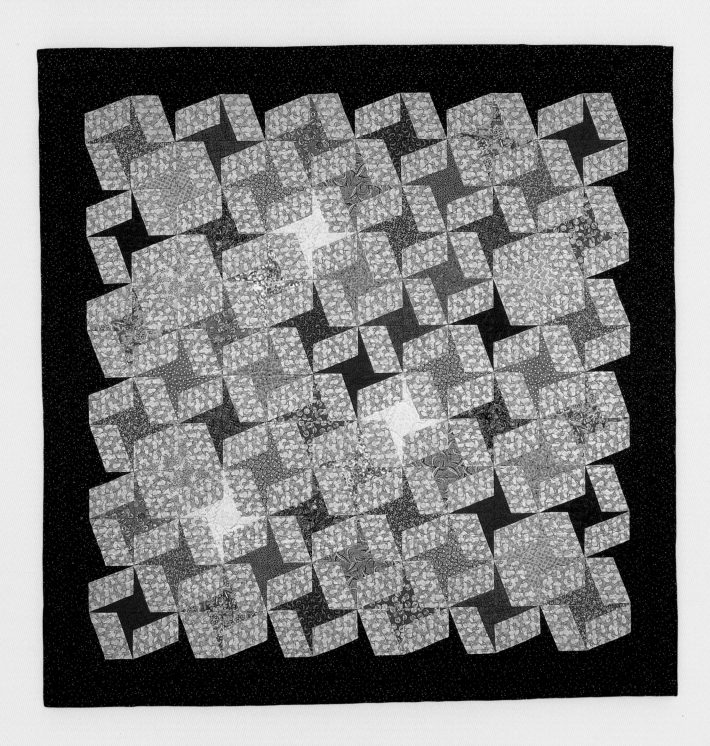

"Sean's Stars" by Jean M. Potetz, 77½" x 77½", Granby, Connecticut.
Machine quilted by Wilma Cogliantry.

SCRAP-FILLED STARS upon a field of blue—these Endless Stars would bring a little sunshine into any room of your house. Comprised of 25 fabrics, "Sean's Stars" requires thought and organization, but watching its colorful stars emerge as the rows are sewn together is ample reward for time spent in the planning stage.

Fabric Guide

Organizing your fabrics for this quilt is easier when you separate the main-star fabrics (1–12) from the secondary-star fabrics (13–25) by color, value, texture, and scale. I used my brighter fabrics for the main stars and the slightly more subdued shades and textures for the secondary stars. This balanced the quilt and, because the main and secondary star fabrics were of different styles, helped me keep my main and secondary stars separate. The bright red secondary star in the center uses a vibrant main star fabric to draw the eye inward. Border stars are made of the same deep navy print as the border, framing the scrappy stars in an interesting border design. For additional advice about fabric selection, read "Endless Stars Fabrics" on page 7.

Finished Quilt: 77½" x 77½" • **Star Unit:** 6"

Materials

Yardage is based on 42"-wide fabric.

- ½ yard of red print for (main) star 1 (corner stars)
- ⅓ yard of purple print for (main) star 2
- ⅓ yard of green print for (main) star 3
- ⅓ yard of dark blue print for (main) star 4
- ½ yard of gold print for (main) star 5
- ½ yard of red print for (main) star 6 (corner stars) and (secondary) star 19 (center star)
- ⅓ yard of blue print for (main) star 7
- ⅓ yard of black print for (main) star 8
- ⅓ yard of gold print for (main) star 9
- ¼ yard of green print for (main) star 10
- ⅓ yard of brown print for (main) star 11
- ¼ yard of purple print for (main) star 12
- ¼ yard of gold print for (secondary) star 13
- ¼ yard of tan print for (secondary) star 14

- ¼ yard of green print for (secondary) star 15
- ¼ yard of gold print for (secondary) star 16
- ½ yard of red print for (secondary) star 17
- ⅓ yard of tan print for (secondary) star 18
- ¼ yard of gold print for (secondary) star 20
- ⅓ yard of tan print for (secondary) star 21
- ¼ yard of purple print for (secondary) star 22
- ¼ yard of green print for (secondary) star 23
- ¼ yard of red print for (secondary) star 24
- 3⅓ yards of navy print for (border) star 25, borders, and binding*
- 4 yards of medium blue print for background
- 7½ yards for backing
- 82" x 82" piece of batting
- 6"-square ruler

If you want to select your border fabric after you have completed the star units, purchase 1 yard of navy print, 1⅔ yards of border fabric, and ⅔ yard of binding fabric.

Cutting

Cut all strips across the full width of the fabric (selvage to selvage). All measurements include ¼" seam allowance.

Main Stars

From the red print star 1 fabric, cut:
– 4 strips, 2½" x 42"

From the purple print star 2 fabric, cut:
– 3 strips, 2½" x 42"

From the green print star 3 fabric, cut:
– 3 strips, 2½" x 42"

From the dark blue print star 4 fabric, cut:
– 3 strips, 2½" x 42"

From the gold print star 5 fabric, cut:
– 4 strips, 2½" x 42"

From the red print star 6 and (secondary) star 19 fabric, cut:
– 4 strips, 2½" x 42"; crosscut 4 rectangles, 2½" x 8", from 1 strip (for star 19)

From the blue print star 7 fabric, cut:
– 3 strips, 2½" x 42"

From the black print star 8 fabric, cut:
– 3 strips, 2½" x 42"

From the gold print star 9 fabric, cut:
– 3 strips, 2½" x 42"

From the green print star 10 fabric, cut:
– 2 strips, 2½" x 42"

From the brown print star 11 fabric, cut:
– 3 strips, 2½" x 42"

From the purple print star 12 fabric, cut:
– 2 strips, 2½" x 42"

Secondary Stars

From the gold print star 13 fabric, cut:
– 2 strips, 2½" x 42"; crosscut 8 rectangles, 2½" x 8"

From the tan print star 14 fabric, cut:
– 1 strip 2½" x 42"; crosscut 4 rectangles, 2½" x 8"

From the green print star 15 fabric, cut:
– 2 strips, 2½" x 42"; crosscut 8 rectangles, 2½" x 8"

From the gold print star 16 fabric, cut:
– 2 strips, 2½" x 42"; crosscut 8 rectangles, 2½" x 8"

From the red print star 17 fabric, cut:
– 4 strips, 2½" x 42"; crosscut 16 rectangles, 2½" x 8"

From the tan print star 18 fabric, cut:
– 3 strips, 2½" x 42"; crosscut 12 rectangles, 2½" x 8"

From the gold print star 20 fabric, cut:
– 1 strip 2½" x 42"; crosscut 4 rectangles, 2½" x 8"

From the tan print star 21 fabric, cut:
– 3 strips, 2½" x 42"; crosscut 12 rectangles, 2½" x 8"

From the purple print star 22 fabric, cut:
– 2 strips 2½" x 42"; crosscut 8 rectangles, 2½" x 8"

From the green print star 23 fabric, cut:
– 2 strips 2½" x 42"; crosscut 8 rectangles, 2½" x 8"

From the red print star 24 fabric, cut:
– 2 strips 2½" x 42"; crosscut 8 rectangles, 2½" x 8"

From the navy print star 25, border, and binding fabric, cut:
– 9 strips, 2½" x 42"; crosscut 44 rectangles, 2½" x 8"
– 8 strips, 6" x 42"; crosscut one 6" square from each strip
– 8 strips, 2" x 42"

Background

From the medium blue background print, cut:
– 36 strips, 3¾" x 42"

Making the Star Units

1. Referring to the row layout diagram on page 57, divide your star fabrics into two groups, main star fabrics 1–12 and secondary star fabrics 13–25. Label a swatch of each fabric with its star number for reference. You will need this information throughout the quilt's assembly. Label your strips and rectangles with star numbers and keep them in separate piles.

2. Sew the 2½" main-star strips to the 3¾" background strips. Keep the strip sets sorted by star number. Press the seam allowances toward the main-star strips as indicated by the arrows in the diagram. Make a total of 36 strip sets.

Make 36 strip sets.

3. Following the strip-set tables, sew the secondary-star rectangles to the background strips as shown. Leave a small gap of approximately ¾" between rectangles. There will be ample fabric for all of the required rectangles. Press seam allowances toward the rectangles.

★ STAR TIP ★

Before you begin sewing, refer to the strip-set tables and compile the secondary-star rectangles required for each set of strip sets. Group each stack of rectangles with its respective strip sets. This step helps eliminate errors and allows for continuous sewing when you are ready to start.

Star 1 Strip Sets

Rectangle	Quantity Needed
13	2
14	1
15	2
16	1
25	10

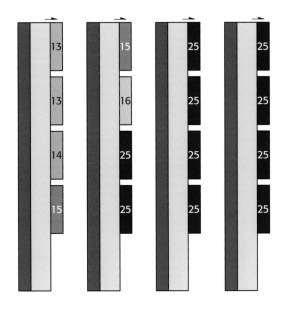

Star 2 Strip Sets

Rectangle	Quantity Needed
13	2
17	3
18	1
19	1
20	1
25	4

Star 3 Strip Sets

Rectangle	Quantity Needed
15	1
16	2
17	1
18	1
21	1
22	1
23	1
25	4

Star 4 Strip Sets

Rectangle	Quantity Needed
18	2
19	1
21	2
22	1
24	2
25	4

Star 5 Strip Sets

Rectangle	Quantity Needed
15	2
16	1
18	1
23	2
24	2
25	8

Star 6 Strip Sets

Rectangle	Quantity Needed
13	1
17	1
18	1
21	1
23	2
25	6

Star 7 Strip Sets

Rectangle	Quantity Needed
13	2
14	1
15	1
16	1
17	1
18	1
20	1
25	4

Star 8 Strip Sets

Rectangle	Quantity Needed
13	1
15	1
16	1
17	3
18	1
21	2
22	2
24	1

Star 9 Strip Sets

Rectangle	Quantity Needed
16	1
17	3
18	1
19	1
21	2
22	2
23	1
24	1

Star 10 Strip Sets

Rectangle	Quantity Needed
17	1
18	1
20	1
21	3
22	1
24	1

Star 11 Strip Sets

Rectangle	Quantity Needed
14	1
17	2
18	1
19	1
21	1
22	1
23	1
25	4

Star 12 Strip Sets

Rectangle	Quantity Needed
14	1
15	1
16	1
17	1
18	1
20	1
23	1
24	1

4. Use a 6"-square ruler to cut 144 star units from the strip sets. Refer to "Cutting Endless Stars Units" on page 9 for detailed instructions. Handle the star units carefully, as they are cut on the fabric's stretchy bias.

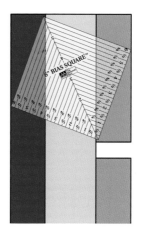

Assembling the Quilt Top

1. Using the row layout diagram below as a guide, carefully arrange the star units into 12 rows. Each row contains 12 star units.

2. Sew the star units in each row together, always sewing like star fabrics together. Use a dry iron to press the seam allowances in the direction indicated by the arrows on the row layout diagram.

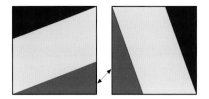

Always sew like star fabrics together.

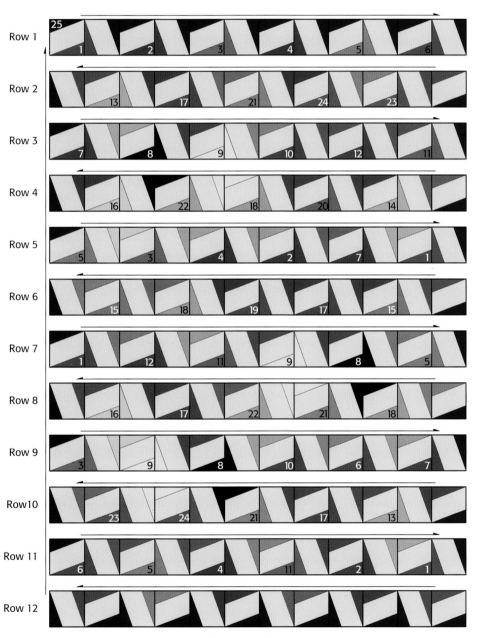

Row Layout Diagram

3. Butting seams to match, pin and sew the rows together. Use a dry iron to press seam allowances toward the top of the quilt.

4. Sew the 6" border strips and 6" corner squares to the quilt. Refer to the instructions for "Borders with Corner Squares" on page 15.

Finishing the Quilt

Refer to "Finishing the Quilt" on page 18 for directions regarding the following steps.

1. Layer the quilt with batting and backing. Baste.

2. Quilt as desired. "Sean's Stars" was machine quilted in a pattern that depicts flying birds.

3. Bind the quilt as described on page 19.

4. Label your quilt.

Quilt Diagram

Cool Confection
By Andrea J. Wysocki, 28" x 28", Suffield, Connecticut.

July Sky Stars
By Jeanne Bennett-Russo, 38" x 38",
Middlefield, Connecticut.

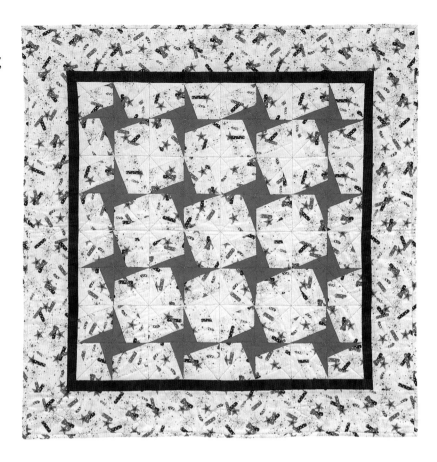

Buddy's Stars
By Susan V. Varesio, 38" x 38",
Bristol, Connecticut.

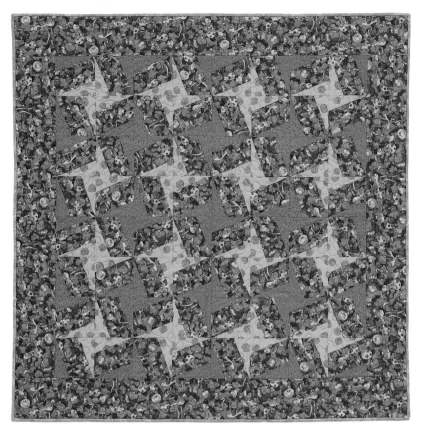

Something's Fishy
By Jean M. Potetz, 35" x 35",
Granby, Connecticut.

Endless Chickens
By Linda Kozlenko, 42" x 42",
Kensington, Connecticut.

Stars and Windmills
By Jean M. Potetz, 34" x 44",
Granby, Connecticut.

Endless Stars
By Linda Kozlenko, 41½" x 51",
Kensington, Connecticut.

Berry Berry Sundae
*By Katherine Kurpiewski, 48" x 48",
Newington, Connecticut.*

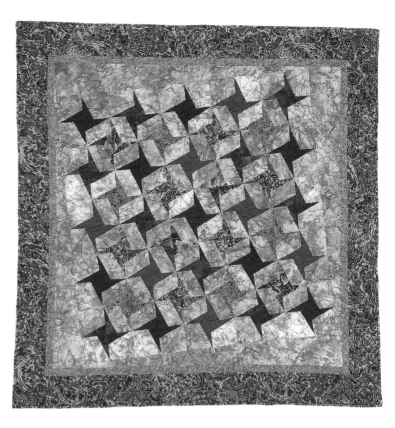

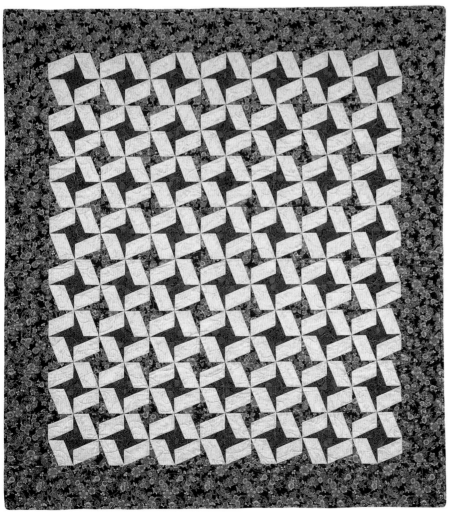

Oriental Evening
*By Jill A. Negrelli, 60" x 67",
Middletown, Connecticut.*

Bibliography

Hanson, Joan, and Mary Hickey. *The Simple Joys of Quilting*.
    Woodinville, Wash.: Martingale & Company, 2001.

Kimball, Jeana. *Loving Stitches, revised edition*.
    Woodinville, Wash.: Martingale & Company, 2003.

Noble, Maurine. *Machine Quilting Made Easy!*
    Woodinville, Wash.: Martingale & Company, 1994.

About the Author

JEAN M. POTETZ made her first quilt in 1975. With little quilting background and without directions, she cut an almost-square template out of cardboard, bought some polyester fabric, and went to work. She's been making quilts ever since, but is pleased to note that her knowledge of quilting and her skills have improved over time.

Interested in old quilts and in preserving their history, Jean repairs quilts and is presently researching a signed quilt from the mid-1800s she rescued from certain destruction. She hopes one day to visit the maker's gravesite and walk the paths she once walked. Jean has participated in the Connecticut Quilt Search Project and is a member of the Salmon Brook Historical Society, where she is working on a textile preservation project.

Most important to her, Jean has "passed the needle" to her daughter, Andrea.

Jean lives in Connecticut's wooded hills with her husband, Richard, and their dogs, Kate and Maggie. Jean and Richard have two grown children. When not quilting, Jean enjoys walking in the woods, gathering pinecones, and feeding the birds in the winter.